Life of Faith

that's my HOUSE

Faith Has the Vision
and God Has the Plan

Includes a scripture journaling section

CHRISTIE AMOYO

THAT'S MY HOUSE
Copyright © 2022 by Christie Amoyo

All rights reserved. Neither this publication nor any part of this publication may be reproduced or transmitted in any form or by any means, electronic or mechanical, including photocopying, recording or any information storage and retrieval system, without permission in writing from the author.

Scriptures taken from the Holy Bible, New International Version®, NIV®. Copyright © 1973, 1978, 1984, 2011 by Biblica, Inc.™ Used by permission of Zondervan. All rights reserved worldwide. www.zondervan.com The "NIV" and "New International Version" are trademarks registered in the United States Patent and Trademark Office by Biblica, Inc.™

Softcover ISBN: 978-1-4866-2223-8
Hardcover ISBN: 978-1-4866-2181-1
eBook ISBN: 978-1-4866-2224-5

Word Alive Press
119 De Baets Street, Winnipeg, MB R2J 3R9
www.wordalivepress.ca

Cataloguing in Publication may be obtained through Library and Archives Canada

Contents

Foreword vii

Introduction ix

Part One

1. The Washer and Dryer 1
2. That's Your House 9
3. She Touched My Heart 13
4. Faith Stretch 19
5. Time to Move! 23
6. A New Season 27
7. Moving Forward 33
8. More than We Could Ask For 39
9. Exercising Yet Again! 45
10. Blessed Life 51
11. Back to Basics 59
12. Double Portion 65

Part Two

13. God's Word Over Our Finances 73

I want to dedicate this book to my husband, Danrey. I thank him for running with the vision that God put on our hearts and living this life of faith together.

"Let us not become weary in doing good, for at the proper time we will reap a harvest if we do not give up" (Galatians 6:9, NIV).

Foreword

Everyone will be able to love and appreciate the wisdom in this book. As a professional life, business, and financial coach myself, I can tell you that there are a lot of lessons that inspire me from these chapters. The book presents more than just regular "information." It will give you something to live by.

I have admired Pastor Christie Amoyo since she was a youth volunteer at my church. Ever since hearing her on stage for the first time, I have known that she continuously uses her life, talents, and abilities to inspire, encourage, and uplift anyone who is ready.

Pastor Christie is not just an encourager; she is also a leader with an open mind and heart to learn from successful visionaries. She believes that God has orchestrated everyone in her life to play the part that they do.

What I can say about this book? This is a must-read!

Do not wait for your situations to change. That's the guiding principle of this book, which is based on real-life experience. This should be one of your go-to books, especially when you're doubting your ability to conquer the trials and challenges in your life.

As an author myself, I am passionate about learning from the contributions of other authors like Pastor Christie, who has dedicated herself to bringing out the best in people. She and I share the same faith and vision.

In my very real conversations with Pastor Christie, I have been able to share with her my views on how to pursue life while continuously engaging and adding value to my clients, friends, and family through my books, corporate sessions, and on-stage life coaching. From the spark in her eyes, I have seen that she is called to lead, write, and speak about her stories.

By reading this book, you will have a connection with a true servant leader who is willing to take you where your life is meant to be. I encourage you to discover what you may be able to learn from this book. You will surely love all the faith stories!

Don't take my word for it. I want you to dedicate your time to learning from this book and encourage others to do the same.

—Coach Clarissa Calingasan
I.M.A.G.E. Transformation Success Coach
www.connectwithcoachclarissa.com

Introduction

When we started to live a life of faith—real faith, not just religious belief—our whole world opened up. Things we had previously thought were impossible to believe for became attainable. They were just waiting for us! If the vision that rises up in you scares you and makes you question how you could even do that, then you know it's from God. Only through Him can you do all things.

My husband and I were in religion, worked so hard for many years, and didn't see anything great happen in our lives. We made the most of what we could do, but all the pressures on us just kept weighing us down. We loved God and knew we wanted to work in the church and minister to people whenever we got the chance. We believed that God had placed that desire in us. So we went to Bible College and did the work—putting in long hours and pouring every ounce of our energy into ministry.

Ministry is a good thing. But when doing those things—good, religious things—took us away from listening to God for our own lives, we realized that we were doing something wrong.

It's great when people want to get involved in church and mission trips and all that, but we can really disconnect from ourselves when the pressures start to come. We've been told for so long that God needs our service, that He needs us to sacrifice and work hard for the Kingdom. Which is true. But He also wants that to come out of our relationship with Him.

We need to come first. Our relationship with God on a personal level is the most important thing. When we spend time with Him first, we are happy to help the body of Christ wherever God leads us. We are to give God our best and listen to the Holy Spirit in order for our service to be pleasing to Him. When we do this, we won't feel like we're losing anything through our sacrifices. Our hard work will be filled with passion!

When your priorities are right, it becomes so easy to walk out *real* faith. We take the pressure off ourselves and place our lives in God's mighty hands, choosing to agree with Him.

Faith is an action word. In religious circles, we've heard too often that just going to church means we have faith. The truth is that going to church doesn't please God. Having faith does. When we have real faith, going out and doing ministry becomes exciting. And we won't lose our focus along the way.

We may say that we believe in Jesus. That's the first step in faith. But then what? If you believe in Him, you should believe that His Word is true. And if you believe that His Word is true, you should be walking it out. That's what faith is: agreeing with God's Word and bringing it into your world.

Today, we're still on the journey of learning to walk by faith first in every area of our lives. I write this book to encourage you to just take the first step. As you do, more opportunities will come to you and more doors will open. Most importantly, your own vision and destiny will become visible to you. God only asks us to trust Him.

God cares about the things we care about, whether it be spiritual, physical, or financial. Sometimes we think we shouldn't talk about the financial aspects of our Christian walk, but what if that's the avenue where you first have experienced the results of stepping out in faith? You take what you've learned in that situation and apply it to the next area of your life where you want to see God's hand at work. Soon enough, you end up carrying around a tattered little book of scriptures, knowing that its contents have the power you need. These scriptures become the building blocks of faith in your life as you come to better know and understand God's will, which you can turn to when faced with any and every obstacle. Your vision will increase and your dreams and goals will manifest.

That's how all the things we used to call miracles happened for us. I want to encourage you because I'm just me, but I've experienced many supernatural events in my life while having only the faith of a mustard seed. Miracles are actually God's will happening in our lives. We're supposed to get used to this!

Our finances are a tool we've been blessed with. God cares about every aspect of our lives. He takes care of us, and the dreams He gives us impact everyone around us. If we love God and others, we will see God's provision in our lives. He's got plans for you that only you can fulfil, and you have to let Him provide for you.

If you can't get over the idea that God has great financial provision and blessings in store for you, maybe you need to start with the end of this book first. Read what God says about you and how blessed you are. It will change the way you think!

Part One

chapter one

The Washer and Dryer

I CAN REMEMBER A TIME WHEN WE WERE CONFIDENT IN THE FACT that God was our healer. We had both experienced physical healings and miracles and our minds had been renewed with the Word of God. We had started walking in faith.

After about twelve years of "living for God" and working in ministry, our lives drastically changed. We'd thought that church services and working in ministry meant that God would always take care of us. We thought we should be living in some sort of supernatural abundance and overflow.

Well, it's true that God loves us and watches over us, but our life and finances showed that we didn't understand what His Word said. If the Bible says we're worth more than sparrows and that He has good plans for us, why weren't we seeing very much happen in our lives?

The pit we had dug because of our own ignorance just kept getting deeper. We were growing weary and frustrated by constantly trying to make ends meet while putting smiles on our face as though to prove that God was good.

One day I drove to my mother's house and she had a gift for me. She handed me a set of CDs called *Fixing the Money Thing* by Gary Keesee. I had never even heard of him, but I was definitely interested in the topic.

I introduced these CDs to my husband Danrey as we left for a camping trip at which he had been asked to be the guest speaker. We'd only been invited because it was for his parents' church group. We were just happy to get away for free, especially we'd just come out of our own health battles, he with depression and me having just given birth to our miracle baby.[1] We had seen God do physical miracles in our lives and we couldn't really answer the question of why they had happened.

We put in the first CD, and to our surprise the speaker didn't talk about money right away. Instead he spoke of healing and miracle babies. Really?! That definitely caught our attention and our hearts were open to hear more.

As we listened, we learned more about the Kingdom of God and how finances operate. Those messages didn't just give us some nice encouragement; they gave us actual faith steps we could take.

We were so intrigued by what we were hearing that we didn't want to stop! After we got to the camp, we took every opportunity to listen to those CDs. In fact, a newfound fire and boldness came over Danrey to start preaching about these truths we were still just learning about.

Something was clicking in our heads and hearts. It was the Spirit of God opening us up to know with certainty that He does have a great plan for us, and it includes prosperity in every area of our lives.

When we were leaving that camp, a couple approached us with a gift of money… and it was so much that it caught our

---

[1] For more details on this, look for my previous book, *The Promised Child*.

attention. God was up to something. He was making all things new for us and revealing what we were missing.

Because we had experienced His power physically in our lives, we started to recognize other areas in which we wanted to see change.

One area was our house. I was always able to have a lot of fun making our various houses *homes*. Whether we had the money to purchase the decor I wanted or not, I found ways to personalize our space and make it warm, inviting, and functional. I regularly read home decorating and renovation magazines, cutting out all the pictures I liked. I even sketched out house designs I liked and kept them in my adult doodle books.

> HE WAS MAKING ALL THINGS NEW FOR US AND REVEALING WHAT WE WERE MISSING.

I had always known that this wasn't a waste of time or fleeting fantasy; it was my heart's desire.

When we got to the place in our lives when we were thinking about houses, God started to give us wisdom in our finances. We began to pray about every financial thing that was on our hearts and recognized our prayers being answered with new ideas and new ways of thinking.

Starting a ministry without much money in the bank already felt crazy, but we had done it because God had given us the vision. Literally, our whole thought process changed after we listened to those CDs. Our minds were being renewed and we couldn't help but show people how amazing God is. That's when He showed us to start our own ministry. It would be a leap of faith and a chance to really trust God. We heard Him, saw the vision, and then stepped out!

We knew that God was filling His house with the people and the plan.

At this same time, we were given the opportunity to purchase my parents' home, the home I had grown up in. It fit us just right. We had two children and the home was a spacious two-bedroom. The price was extremely good, too. My parents gave us a great deal!

So within a few short weeks we became homeowners and were enjoying the blessing of God.

Just as God was teaching us about how His Kingdom works, He walked us through what it means to trust Him. He taught us not to worry about things, especially our health and finances, two things that are tangible and physical.

I really appreciate how God chooses to speak to me. I am very simple and need Him to lay things out clearly so I can understand it. As He does this, I am continually amazed at how the Christian life is a simple act of faith; anyone can believe and receive all of God—if they want to.

I got pregnant shortly after we settled into our family home and devised a great plan for how we would all fit nicely in the house. But as I looked in magazines and took road trips outside Winnipeg, the city where we lived, I began to love the idea of living in the countryside. I wanted my kids to have a huge yard and peaceful surroundings.

Danrey and I talked about the areas just outside the city. Some were very close indeed and still allowed for many conveniences, such as remaining close to our children's school.

We now desired to live outside the city. Maybe we could rent out or sell the home we'd just bought.

Of course, this was all just a prayer at that point.

Through this time of starting our own church, moving into our own home, and even building a business on the side, God never stopped teaching us about how to believe Him for all our needs and wants. A lot of people think that God will take care of us, but they warn against getting greedy and asking Him for everything under the sun.

But that's not what I read in the Bible. I'm a tither, and God tells us in Malachi 3:10:

> *Bring the whole tithe into the storehouse, that there may be food in my house. Test me in this... and see if I will not throw open the floodgates of heaven and pour out so much blessing that there will not be room enough to store it.*

What kind of blessing is God talking about here? Whatever it is, it sounded like a good thing to me.

I later read in Luke 6:38,

> *Give, and it will be given to you. A good measure, pressed down, shaken together and running over, will be poured into your lap. For with the measure you use, it will be measured to you.*

I'm a giver, too. I enjoy giving to my church and various projects, not to mention helping anyone in need. Here, God says that because I am a giver, I will receive!

So I started to get specific with my prayers. I gave my tithes at church but then also gave extra offerings, being encouraged to write down the things I was praying for. As I gave, I would call each prayer done and answered. My faith was in my God, and now my giving was connected to my faith as well.

I gave extra and expected God to do things that I couldn't. Because I believed that I was going to see God move more and more in my life, I did! I began to see His provision more and more.

Again, I am very simple and God needs to speak to me very clearly. One day, my dryer just stopped working. I was only on the first load of what seemed like a million loads that day, so I wasn't impressed.

I prayed over the dryer. Nothing. I started to speak to it. Nothing. I kicked it. Nothing.

But as I hung up all of my wet clothes, I got the idea to sow a seed, an offering, into the church and ask God for a new dryer. I felt silly but excited all at the same time.

When Danrey came home, he saw the silly look on my face; let's call it *faith face*. By the time I told him the story, I had changed my prayer a bit and asked him to agree with me in prayer. We agreed to sow a $50 seed and believe God to give us a brand-new washer and dryer. You heard me: I wanted both!

Within a few days, I got really getting frustrated with having to hang up the wet clothes. But I was also teaching myself to thank God through it all and I continued thanking Him for my new washer and dryer.

After a few days passed, while walking past the dryer, I pressed the on button—and it worked!

Praise God, I thought. *He made my dryer work!*

I put in a load of clothes, thanking God for fixing my dryer, but I reminded Him that I had sowed my seed for a brand new washer and dryer and I wasn't giving up on receiving them just because the dryer was working again. And I was very specific and stubborn, telling God that I wanted the new front-loading kind.

My dryer worked for the next nine months, and every time I used it I thanked God for my brand-new washer and dryer.

Then, suddenly, it stopped working again one day. I got excited and thought this must be the time for my new washer and dryer. I could have financed a new washer and dryer at any point during those nine months, but I hadn't been willing to compromise. I didn't want to go into debt. I wanted to be a part of something cool that God was doing in my life.

That week, I got an excited call from my aunt who works at a second-hand store. She told me that they had received a front-loading Maytag washer and dryer, and immediately she'd thought of me. She could give them to me for $500. So did I want them? Absolutely!

I knew they were mine, but there was only one problem. I didn't have $500.

I had a gift of $300 coming to me that week, so I at least had some of the money. So I decided to just expect God to provide the rest. I am His daughter and He takes care of His children!

That very day, I spoke on the phone to my grandmother. When I told her about the new washer and dry, she was so excited about it that she offered to contribute the final $200. Wow!

Some people may not understand how excited I was about this. After all, it's just a washer and dryer, but I was amazed at how God provided what I needed and wanted, the best of its kind. For nine months I'd kept thanking Him for something I could have gone out the very next day and financed on my own. But I wanted to see Him do it His way! No stress, no fear, no debt, no worry. It's fun to see His hand orchestrate it all.

chapter two

That's Your House

God moved in our lives in amazing ways during that time, but we were still longing for our home outside the city. The opportunity presented itself at church one day when we were able to give a large seed of $10,000. When we gave this money, we both prayed in our hearts to receive our home outside the city. It was really exciting to write that down and begin to thank God for it regularly.

By this time in our lives, our third child was just over a year old and the house was getting pretty tight. We had heard of many great testimonies of God providing houses for people, blessing them with opportunities to own land, so we knew that if we believed and had patience He would open that door for us. And we knew it would be better than we could even imagine!

Around this time, my brother was selling his house. He too was contemplating moving outside the city. We often talked about our favourite spots, and I told him that I loved the area around the nearby town of Lorette. That's where I wanted to be. At my previous job, the boss had driven in to work from his house in Lorette and it had only taken him ten minutes. I thought that was a perfect distance.

Well, my brother and his family ended up selling their home and finding a house in Lorette. Now he was waiting for us to come there, too!

We actively looked at homes around the city, specifically around Lorette. We loved the thought of having a big yard and a few acres. I think my longing to raise our family in the country, and having family gatherings there, came from memories of my amma (grandma) who had lived on a farm when I was little. I'd always loved travelling out of the city, enjoying the fresh air and the peace and love of having the family around.

One day we went to my brother's house for dinner, and when we got there he told us about a house that had just come on the market. He really wanted to take us to see it. The property had five acres and two homes. It was way out of our price range, but we wanted to dream big.

When we got to the property, which was also only five minutes away from my brother's house, we found a large older home with an attached mobile home in the back. The main house had five bedrooms. I love ceiling beams, big windows, and neat character rooms and spaces—and this house definitely had all of that! And without going outside you could get into the mobile home through a breezeway. We entered the mobile home to find that it had a great setup as well, with three additional bedrooms. The property also had a huge garage/workshop with tons of storage room, enough to park a semitruck.

As the days passed, I thought of all the fun things we could do with that house. I imagined decorating it using ideas from all the magazines I'd seen. And although we looked at many houses with my brother, none of them stood out like that one.

But we really didn't have the finances to do anything. All we could do was pray and wait.

That's Your House

While I was at home one day, listening to a teaching from Jesse Duplantis, a certain sentence he spoke hit me hard: "You've been thinking about that house because it's your house!" I jumped to my feet, my heart pounding, and agreed with him: "Yes, that is my house!"

Immediately I looked up the house online… but I couldn't find it. I called my brother and asked him why the house wasn't listed anymore and he said that it hadn't sold. He didn't know why it was off the market.

Danrey came home from work that day and I practically attacked him at the door. I told him that this house in Lorette was ours. We were going to drive out there and knock on the door. He thought I was crazy, and you may think the same, but my spirit was stirred up and nothing was going to stop me.

> HE THOUGHT I WAS CRAZY, AND YOU MAY THINK THE SAME, BUT MY SPIRIT WAS STIRRED UP AND NOTHING WAS GOING TO STOP ME.

He saw the excitement in my eyes and agreed to drive out with me and do it. We prayed and praised God throughout the drive, not really having a plan except to just knock on the door.

When we got there, I ran out of the van and knocked on the door… and no one answered. I went back to the van and wrote a note, asking the owners if they were still interested in selling their home. I left my phone number on the piece of paper.

Within a few days, I did get a phone call back—but it wasn't what I was expecting to hear. To be honest, I didn't know what to expect. My faith had told me it was time to move some mountains and get into this house.

My mind was a battlefield of questions. Were the people going to call back? Would they even want to talk to me? What would I say if they wanted to sell? Where was that large amount of money actually going to come from? Would God send someone to purchase it for us… like an angel? I've heard many amazing testimonies of God providing for people in supernatural ways.

At the same time, I also questioned whether this was God speaking to my spirit. Was it Him, or was it just what I wanted to hear?

chapter three

She Touched My Heart

I HAD WAITED FOR DAYS TO RECEIVE THIS PHONE CALL, SO WHEN my phone rang with an unknown number, I hoped it would be someone calling to tell me some news about the house. The woman on the phone explained that she had found my note—and yes, they were still interested in selling their property.

But there had been a change in their plans. Through sniffles and tears, she told me that her husband had just passed away, which is why they had pulled the house off the market. What I didn't expect was for us to talk for another twenty minutes about the amazing man her husband had been. She didn't know why God would allow him to get sick and pass away.

This opened the door for me to comfort her. She really needed someone to talk to, and soon she discovered that my husband and I were pastors. Our conversation bounced back and forth from the house plans and current events to her husband. I could feel that her heart so torn.

We decided to set up a date for us to come see the house again, this time with our kids.

I was anxious about the thought of going out there, but I also had a crazy amount of confidence that God was setting something up. In the days leading up to the visit, every scripture of God's provision rattled through my head. I knew we couldn't afford the property in the natural, but I remained confident that God would show me what to do.

A few days later, we took our two older children out to see "our house." We were so grateful to meet our now family friend, Dorothy. She was there with her son-in-law to show us around the property again and then to sit with us to discuss the details of the purchase. They made us feel so welcome, and our kids were right at home on her sofa watching cartoons.

We let her know that we loved the house, and it fit our situation perfectly, as we intended to live very close to our parents. She knew we didn't have all the finances in place at the moment, but we were all willing to take some steps and see if we could make it work.

Before we had left, I was also able to pass on a page of healing scriptures that I had made for her. Over the phone, she had let me know of some health concerns she was starting to have, since her doctor had mentioned some cancer.

I was grateful that she was so open and willing to work with us, but I was also grateful that she would open up to me so I could pray for her.

One month went by and we talked further. I wanted God to move quickly and show us how to get in there before Christmas. But by October we weren't any closer to our goal. I started to feel really nervous as we talked to Dorothy and I had nothing further to tell her.

We went to the bank and told them of our plans, hoping they could advise us on the next steps to take. I was never happy going to the bank. Even though we had been good homeowners, they just kept telling us we didn't make enough money. My heart for this purchase was to see God's hand move. I knew He didn't want us to be in debt with this house... but I also knew, based on how He had provided for us before, He would do it again.

It also turned out that my parents wouldn't be able to move in with us yet. My mother lived in the same apartment block as my grandmother and she took care of her every day. Grandma was starting to need extra help.

We took my husband's parents out to look at the house, to see if they would be interested in living out there with us. But they, too, had different plans.

One night in November, I lay on the bed in tears, asking God what I was supposed to say to Dorothy when she called next. I didn't like that I had no answers and hadn't made any progress. In fact, I felt like God was being silent.

Then the phone rang.

"Well, can you buy the house now?" Dorothy said in a strong voice.

I gulped and told her with a sigh that I didn't have anything to give her. I told her to hold onto my phone number in case her plans changed. Her voice softened and she said that she wasn't even sure she wanted to move right at this point; this had been her and her husband's and she may not be ready to let it go just yet anyway.

We ended up talking longer and she thanked me for the scriptures I had given her. When we ended our conversation, we were filled with peace and hope.

I was speechless when I hung up. I felt sure that I had been ready to give up my house, to completely let it go, only for Dorothy to give me so much grace and a renewed sense of hope.

God was still up to something.

Leading up to Christmas, I grabbed my book of provision scriptures as often as I could. I read over the verses, knowing that I needed to keep filling up on faith and believing that God would work things out.

Christmas came and went and I could only imagine what it would be like to celebrate in that beautiful home. My home!

For months and months, I dreamt about being in that home and raising our family there. I picked out the paint for each room and even planned where the furniture would go. I didn't know it at the time, but Danrey was doing the same thing with the garage, counting how many cars he could collect in it.

> GOD WAS STILL UP TO SOMETHING.

As we continued to with the work of our church and our business, many doors of opportunity opened up. We knew that when we sowed seeds of faith for our house, God was going to show us how and where to harvest.

I talked with Dorothy every few weeks and we had lots to be excited about. Knowing that we needed to make some money to purchase the home and live comfortably there, she continually gave us advice on how to bring in more income.

In the spring, she let me know about her latest doctor's visits. Apparently he had asked about what was happening in her life to make her so cheerful and hopeful. She explained to him about our families working together to buy her home. He even confirmed to her that this must be a great thing, since her health was benefitting from it.

Yep, that's God!

During this season, as we worked hard to gather more income, our relationship with her and her family began to grow.

chapter four

Faith Stretch

By the time summer hit, I found out that I was pregnant again. Our third child was a year and a half old, and now I would be due at Christmas. I was really excited, but now I was also stressed about the house situation. No doubt we needed out of our current house and into a larger home. Fitting six people into two bedrooms definitely wasn't going to work.

When I told Dorothy I was pregnant, she just laughed and celebrated with me. I told her that God had to do something now for us to get into her home. It had to be time.

However, my grandmother had just passed away and life seemed to be moving a little too fast. My emotions were hard hit. I have to be honest: I may have said more complaining prayers to God regarding our house than praise prayers.

I had to remember the words of Mark 11:24, which says, *"Therefore I tell you, whatever you ask for in prayer, believe that you have received it, and it will be yours."* And I partnered this with 1 John 5:14–15:

> *This is the confidence we have in approaching God: that if we ask anything according to his will, he hears us. 15 And if we know that he hears us—whatever we ask—we know that we have what we asked of him.*

God hears our prayers and answers them. I could have confidence that He was working it out, and I believed that I had received it when I asked God for it.

But this pressure on me was bigger than the washer and dryer story. I had someone calling and asking when things were going to happen. Banks were denying our requests for loans and people thought we were nuts for trying to work out this private deal. And all through this, we had our church ministry to think about.

We had to learn a lot in a very short period of time.

I've come to realize that it's okay not to pray about every single thing or always explain your situation to the people around you. Let's face it: not everyone is going to understand or agree with your decisions. This is why it's so important to grow your faith, so you can build up the boldness and courage to stand on your own two feet and know that you know that you know that God is working all things out for your good!

That period of our lives was like an emotional rollercoaster, and it was hard to wait and remain certain about our future and our choices. But Isaiah 55:9 says that His ways are higher than our ways. I just needed to trust Him.

God had only just begun the process of building our foundation of faith. Since starting our church a few years prior, we had already seen so many prayers answered and miracles performed around us. Sometimes it felt easy to have faith. But only when you're faced again and again with challenges do you remember to never let down your guard. We really have to fight the good fright of faith (1 Timothy 6:12).

We were working hard to improve our church's financial standing as we went from renting one location to another. Our congregation was growing both in number and in faith. We were so busy stabilizing our situation that thoughts of the house took a back seat.

Soon enough, summer was over and I began to nest in our current home. It was kind of nice to know I would have all four of our children in the family home where I had grown up.

However, Dorothy knew that if we didn't do this deal now, we would have to wait through another winter. Her property had a lot of space that would have to be taken care of, and her daughter and family would have to find another home quickly if they had to move.

My heart sank as I realized I would have to tell her again that we still weren't able to make the purchase.

And then the phone rang. Dorothy began by expressing that she wanted us to purchase the property now, but then she changed her tone of voice and told me that springtime is when we would need to figure it out.

> IF THE DREAM YOU HAVE IS DOABLE ON YOUR OWN, THEN IT DOESN'T REQUIRE GOD.

We kept believing and knowing that God was doing a great work, even if we didn't yet see the results we wanted.

As Christians who have faith and hope in God, we can get discouraged when our timing isn't His timing. I definitely know that if God hadn't put in my spirit that this was my house, I would have given up on believing for it.

If the dream you have is doable on your own, then it doesn't require God. We need to remember that we need God in everything. We need to stop relying on the things we can do on our own. When we dream bigger, it requires us to use our faith—and without faith, it's impossible to please God (Hebrews 11:6).

On December 30, we welcomed our fourth child, and third son, into this world. Our house was growing smaller by the minute!

chapter five

Time to Move!

As we got into the new routines of school, church, and taking care of another baby, our moving plans grew closer and closer. Spring went by in a blur and before long it was summer again.

I mean, really. It must be time now, right, God?! Dorothy told us that now was the time to get this deal done, and I totally agreed.

We started to get our house ready by packing boxes and getting rid of things we didn't need anymore. Although we were cleaning, prepping, and purging, we still didn't have a clear plan. But it takes action to move in faith, so we decided that our best next step would be to sell our home.

We were given the opportunity to take over Dorothy's mortgage and make extra payments on top of the mortgage to cover the eventual down-payment. It's just that we weren't sure how much the down-payment would be. But we would soon have money from the sale of our home and we figured that everything was going to work out right when we needed it to.

Our realtor, who happened to my brother, listed our home in September and we began to pray for a good sale. We listed the house for top price, which some people told us we wouldn't get.

Despite setting up the house as best we could, the open house didn't go over very well. Only a few people came out to see it. We then had an opportunity to lower the price, but Danrey and I prayed and were convinced that we shouldn't lower the price.

Then, at the beginning of the second week on the market, we had a showing and an immediate offer. The house sold for the price we had asked for.

Now we had one month to move. Or rather, *God* had one month to move.

When we finally got all the paperwork and finances taken care of, we went to Dorothy and began to figure out the details. Everything was going well—until we got to the down-payment. The number that worked for us was too low for her.

Now what?

By this time, I was an emotional wreck. I questioned God. I was really confused as to why things weren't working out. I lay on my bed, having only two weeks to move, and cried. I had to leave my home, my family home, and I didn't know where we would go.

I had allowed Satan to steal my joy and felt so lost.

> I HAD ALLOWED SATAN TO STEAL MY JOY AND FELT SO LOST.

Had I missed God somewhere? I had thought this was my house to move into. I'd thought that I had to take action steps to bring my faith into reality. I'd thought He would direct me along the right path. I'd thought I was hearing His voice…

At our church, He seemed to be pouring out His wisdom and power. In fact, He was showing Himself strongly in every other area of my life. So why not this one?

We had to move... but where were we to go?

My in-laws had a larger home, and now that my husband's siblings had moved out there would be plenty of room for us. That seemed to be our best option.

There were many things I didn't like about moving there. First of all, we had to move our things into a storage locker. The house was also far from the kids' school, and I felt like a failure as my kids had to adjust to that.

Finally, I didn't know my in-laws too well. Our dog was really big, clumsy, and messy and I was always scared she or the kids would break something. I didn't want to get in the way, but that was extremely difficult now that I had a baby and wasn't working. I was the one in the house most days, a house not my own, and I constantly felt like we were a burden.

Eventually I came to realize is that these things which at first seemed like burdens would soon turn into blessings.

chapter six

A New Season

I DIDN'T THINK GOD WANTED TO USE THIS SEASON OF MY LIFE TO give me a new vision and help me enjoy my new surroundings. When you're too focussed on the plans at hand and the goals you're running towards, they can become all you think about. They consume you and cause you to miss out on some important character-building situations.

It was hard to only take a few things with us to our in-laws' house. We brought all our clothes and basic necessities, but we missed having the other comforts of home. But there was no way we could live in a two-bedroom house anymore.

Over time, the long drives to and from the in-laws' house became extremely daunting. It was just so far from everything I knew. That said, the longer drive gave Danrey an opportunity to help out by picking up his mother every day from work. Our children started going to a jujitsu class that was nearer to their house, and they loved it. Even I started to enjoy the shopping amenities close by. We had to make many adjustments, but they lived in a beautiful area, and it gave me the chance to connect with nearby members of my family I normally didn't see too often.

I also got to get to know my in-laws more, which was a blessing on both sides. The way you really get to know someone is by living with them, and I got to connect with my mother-in-law and hear her stories of how it had been to move from the Philippines to Canada with her son and without my father-in-law. She had lived with her husband's family, and it hadn't been easy. Hearing these stories was hard and I ached for her. We don't know what other people have gone through unless we get the chance to walk in their shoes.

The great challenge and testimony of my in-laws is the story of their daughter being close to death when she was young. I listened to my mother-in-law speak of her regrets about how she raised her other two children. As a mother, I imagined myself in her situations. God is so good; He has shown Himself to be strong in their family then and now. He is in the business of restoration.

With us living there, we could see God restoring the family and bringing them so much healing and peace.

During this season, I went through a major shift when God showed me a vision. As I prayed and talked to God one day, I stood on the promise of owning our own home and declared His goodness. As I asked Him to work everything out, I heard Him say to me, "That's your house. Now write your book."

What? My book?

I had always wanted to write a book about the trials of faith we'd experienced through pregnancy loss, as well as the hope, healing, and blessings of having our four children. A spark ignited within me. I got excited about this idea, and also nervous about the challenge of it.

I managed to find time to write when the children went to bed and Danrey was out playing basketball. *The Promised Child* didn't take too long to complete. I was so consumed with the thoughts and plans of writing that the months flew by as we stayed with my in-laws.

I also continued to have many conversations with Dorothy while we lived there. She kept telling me things like how she was sitting in *my* living room right then doing her quilting. She would tell me about the hot water tank she had to replace, getting a bigger one that would be really beneficial for our family. She also got most of the windows replaced. She was super encouraging. There was even a time when she told me that she was going to buy new furniture and that I could keep some of the old items.

> Through it all, I stood on the word that God had given me.

Life was very demanding. There were a lot of things going on in our ministry and family life. Through it all, I stood on the word that God had given me. When I finished writing my book and getting it published, I then said to Him, "Okay, where's my house?"

Even though Dorothy and I kept talking about the plans for the house, we still couldn't come up with a workable solution. We were all kind of stuck about it. I wasn't giving up hope.

The thing that touched me the most, and confirmed that God was still in this, was when she called one morning about a dream she'd had. The dream had been so real and she said she would never forget it. She vividly remembered answering the front door and seeing me there with a bunch of people ready to move our things in. She confidently told me that something was about to happen; the dream had been so real that she felt it must have come from God.

Danrey and I were greatly encouraged to hear about the dream, since we could see that it wouldn't work to continue living with his parents. We needed more space, our own space.

In the meantime, he had seen a nice home for rent in a great area of the city. It had four bedrooms, a large yard, and a finished open basement. It was also close to many stores and parks.

The owner of those home was really nice, but he was concerned that we had a dog. We didn't hear from him for about two weeks because of this… but then he called us. He said that he liked our family, and because our dog was old and I was a stay-at-home mom he would allow us to move in. We moved a couple of weeks after that. It was nice to finally be in a house that fit us!

We didn't plan on being in that house too long, but God was teaching me to enjoy where we were even if we weren't where we wanted to be. I took that to heart. To make it real, I decided to open a new set of dishes we had been given for Christmas a few years earlier. I had been saving them for when we moved into "our house," but right now I needed something pretty and encouraging. I wanted to enjoy the season we were in.

I also found this to be true in other ways. I started to put up decorations in our new home, and even followed up on opportunities to get some new furniture.

We are blessed—not just when we get the things we pray for, but in our everyday lives as we live in God's blessings. I had to learn to appreciate the things we had and be content with them.

But I never gave up hope for believing that we would soon be in our acreage outside the city.

We declared the following passage from Deuteronomy:

When the Lord your God brings you into the land he swore to your fathers, to Abraham, Isaac and Jacob, to give you—a land with large, flourishing cities you did not build, houses filled with all kinds of good things you did not provide, wells you did not dig, and vineyards and olive groves you did not plant...
—Deuteronomy 6:10–11

Probably because we were so focussed on the part about the houses we did not build, we didn't realize until later that God was filling up the house we already had!

One day, a man from our church came up to me with some news. His mother had recently passed away, leaving him with a beautiful china cabinet that he wanted me to have. I received it with great excitement.

Another time, a friend who lived down the street from me was giving away her beautiful king-sized bed. It was too plush and squishy for them. Our bed wasn't very good and I leapt at her offer. This wasn't a bed we would have purchased in the store, as we would have thought it was too squishy as well, but it was way better than what we had and so we decided to give it a chance. We have never regretted that. It's the best bed we've ever had!

Not long after the new bed came, other friends got rid of their living room couch and loveseat. They wanted us to have it. The pieces fit perfectly in our living room!

I remembered my grandmother once telling me something prophetic and humorous before she passed away. She said, "Christie, you're going to have your bed, your couch, and your fridge full of money!" Well, it was coming to pass.

After receiving the bed and the couches, I asked God what it meant to have a fridge full of money. That part I still didn't understand—and wouldn't until a few years later.

When COVID pandemic eventually hit and everything was shut down, I had the opportunity to work from home and home-school my kids.

During this time, I had some single mom friends who needed help with their children. One of those children was being home-schooled with my own kids and stayed at our house a few times a week. Another got dropped off every now and then due to daycare closures.

In gratitude for my help, my friends constantly brought over food in thanks for me watching their children. I would look into my fridge most days and find it overflowing with food. My family was provided for over and above.

God always confirms His word. He will take care of us—always.

chapter seven

Moving Forward

We didn't plan to rent for very long and we told the owner that maybe we would stay as long as a full year. By now, my parents had grown accustomed to the idea of moving with us and staying in the extra home on the property. With the passing of my grandmother, they had decided not to renew the lease on their current apartment. Since they were already coming over to watch our children a lot, they moved in with us. We had enough room and got excited about moving to the acreage in the springtime.

That summer, I got a surprising phone call from Dorothy. She wanted us to officiate her upcoming wedding in November. I was so excited for her; after all, we had first met her after her husband had passed away. She also was in the process of moving some of her things out of the house, since she would be joining her husband in his home after the wedding.

We saw that things for lining up for all of us.

When November came around, it was such an honour and blessing to be part of their wedding. I was nervous to meet her family and didn't know what they would think of us, the ones who had been trying to purchase their mother's home for years now. I felt a little ashamed and embarrassed but put a smile on my face and prayed for everything to go better than I thought it would.

The wedding was warm, welcoming, and beautiful. Dorothy made everyone comfortable with her kind smile and genuinely loving personality. What I didn't expect was that her daughter ended up being exactly the same way; she sat down with us at our table and with warm encouragement said that maybe now everything was going to work out. I really appreciated that. It confirmed the goodness of God in the midst of this whole drawn-out house purchase. God works through people.

> God works through people.

God brought us into a family. He didn't just show us their home; He showed us the people who we eventually grew to have a wonderful and surprising relationship with. We went home from that wedding feeling like we were part of their family. Dorothy had always told me that this was true, but now we really knew it!

Before we left the wedding, I was able to pass along a copy of my book to Dorothy. She had known all about me writing it and wanted to read it. She had such hope in our testimony and our future. To this day, she continues to be an encouragement to me.

Dorothy and her husband Dennis ended up coming to our church a couple of times through the winter as they were able. But it was a text message I received from her that impacted me forever. After reading my book—which is about healing, relating mostly to pregnancy and children—she told me that she now believed she was completely healed from cancer and wanted me and my husband to believe with her about it, too!

I cried when I read that message. I was completely overwhelmed and praised God for it. Dorothy was taking better care of herself, enjoying life, and had cast her care over to God. She believed that healing was for her and she had received it! It literally changed her from the inside-out.

The winter months were fun at our house. We had a great time living with Grandma and Papa around. We all had the same goal in mind, and we expected it to work out.

Because we were confident in knowing that God was working all things out for us, we felt enabled to put our focus elsewhere. But every now and then a prophetic word was spoken over us about our new house. We were surrounded by encouraging people who filled us with ideas about how to help make the deal happen. We just needed something to click into place.

In the springtime, the days just flew by. We didn't have a clear plan for completing the purchase, but Dorothy set up a day with us to hatch out the details. She was going to call me, as she was just coming back from having settled into her new home. I was to wait for her call and then drive out together with her to the house.

It was a school day, and by the end of it we still hadn't heard from her.

As we neared our house after picking up the kids, I noticed an eagle flying in the sky. Eagles don't just fly around in Winnipeg unless they're in the zoo. I showed the kids with amazement.

That's when I got a text message from Dorothy: "The house is burning."

My thoughts began to race. Was it really serious? Was everyone okay? Why had she just texted me this...?

I turned to Danrey and quietly passed along the message to him. We just looked at each other, not wanting to alarm the children.

I texted her back and asked if she was okay. About a half-hour later, she called and explained that her daughter's family and pets had made it out of the house, but both homes were burning at the moment.

I was very thankful to hear that everyone was safe, but I couldn't imagine the scene playing out before her eyes. She had to let me go before too long, though, because the firemen had arrived. She assured me that she would talk to me soon.

My heart sank.

I think I just sat in silence all night. It was really hard to believe that both homes were gone. My home was gone.

I tried hard to hide my emotions from my family, but at the end of the night I had to let it all out. I sat with Danrey in bed and cried as we prayed for everyone and everything. I felt like I had just lost my vision. I had envisioned myself and our family living in that home for the past four years… and now that wasn't going to happen. I couldn't believe it.

I didn't know how to deal with all the feelings I experienced over the days that followed. I was in complete disbelief. Hadn't God's hands been in this plan? How could this have happened? The time had finally come for us to move into our new home… only for it to be taken away from us in an instant.

Dorothy called me a few days later and let me know how she and her family were doing. She hadn't moved very many of her belongings to her new husband's home, so she had lost it all. I can't imagine how that felt. All of her memories were there. My heart ached for her.

But what she said next really shocked me. She expressed how bad she felt that I couldn't move into my house. She then told me that the fire had been caused by faulty wiring in the addition that had been built. She told me how happy she was that we hadn't been living there, because that could have been my family needing to get out.

When I got off the phone with her, all the things she had told me rang in my head and my heart. Again I found myself in tears. I had so much to process—all those years of delay after delay, all those years of trying and working so hard, all those years of waiting... they actually did have a purpose. I was overwhelmed by God's protection upon our family.

A few days after the fire, Danrey and I took a drive up to the house to see it for ourselves. The sight was unimaginable. It was a home without walls. The frame still stood in the main house, but very little remained of the other. It made me sick to my stomach. I was sad for them, and sad for us.

When we pray for something and think God isn't hearing, or maybe we just think it's taking too long, we need to have patience and know that God is answering our prayers. There is always a reason for the timing He chooses.

Now, I wasn't immediately filled with peace about it. After all, we were living in a home I hadn't planned on being in for very long, and now I didn't know what to do.

Although I had moments of awe and gratitude for what God had done, I still struggled with feelings of complete loss. My parents were living with us and we were all getting anxious about where to move next.

One day, I remembered what God had told me: "That's your house. Now write your book." I reminded Him of this and asked Him about what was going to happen now that my house was ruined.

In my spirit, I heard His voice: "The house may be ruined, but the plan is not."

chapter eight

More than We Could Ask For

OVER THE NEXT FEW MONTHS, I GOT REGULAR UPDATES FROM Dorothy about their plans for the house and all their insurance hassles. They had a long road ahead of them to rebuild... and I felt like we did, too. We occasionally drove past their home and saw all the beautiful work being done on their property, the new framing and finishes that were going up. They changed the look of the new house and it no longer had the same pull for me. It felt like that whole chapter had closed, but at least I had gotten a great relationship with Dorothy from it.

When I first met Dorothy, she'd had a heavy heart with much pain and sickness. Now she was married, healed, and enjoying life! If that was the main reason for meeting her, than I thanked God for bringing us together and allowing me to be a part of her transformation. That's what listening to God is all about. Things might not work out the way we think, but the outcome is always way better than we imagine when God is involved.

Following the fire, I brought all these healing thoughts and feelings to God. As I did, a song rose in my soul: "It Is Well with My Soul." Isaiah 55:9 says that His ways are higher than our ways, His thoughts higher than our thoughts. In the aftermath of all this loss, my heart still trusted and believed Him. I still had hope.

When we had first started our church, six years prior, we'd been given an opportunity to put forward a financial offering. That was huge for us. On our envelope we wrote "For our home outside the city." I was reminded of this every now and then, and I reminded God of it, too. I knew that I didn't need to remind Him, but talking to Him about it made me feel better.

I had to refocus my faith and realize that complaining to God about the situation wasn't the right approach. As Christians, when we don't have all the answers, we tend to complain. We complain when things don't go our way, or when things don't happen the way we think they should. We also complain when things seem to take too long.

When I feel like everything around me is out of whack, I have to go back to basics. In fact, I should never stray from the basics. I believe God is very easy to understand and His principles are simple. The act of walking them out shows us where our own faith is at.

Now it was time to again sit down with my husband and remember the things we had first prayed about and sowed seeds for. When we sow a financial seed of faith, according to Mark 11:24, we write down the things we are believing to receive. Danrey and I had been training ourselves to do this constantly. We even bought a book and wrote down inside it all the seeds we would sow, along with the scriptures that went along with our faith. We went back to the book when those promises manifested and wrote down what had happened and when. We have to keep our confidence in God and His Word so we can have faith for bigger things and the pressure life can bring.

Together he and I agreed that God is good and gives us the desires of our hearts. We were not going to beg Him for our home outside the city. Instead we would continue to confidently believe that He was doing what He had said He would do.

We decided to sow more seeds into our house prayer. Financially, we had to stand firm in our faith and listen to everything God instructed us to do.

At this time in our lives, our church had moved into its own building, which was really exciting for us. It was a beautiful building, but only half-renovated. So we had lots to do.

That first year in our building was a real day-to-day faith walk. We were challenged mentally, physically, and spiritually, and during this time our prayers in the Spirit went to the next level, as did our worship and passion, leadership and vision. It was the hardest year of our ministry, but I can say that it was the best.

At the end of that year, God gave me a word about "new wine." This is something we read about in the Bible, but the concept penetrated my heart. When a word or phrase sticks out to me, I stop and dive in, needing to unpack what God is saying through it. During this time, He revealed to me more and more about "new wine" and what it means to have new wineskins.

God was going to do something completely new for us, but we were also going to have to adjust and change in order to have this new wine. Our understanding and relationship with God was changing, growing, and evolving in our lives.

So what does this all mean? We can pray and ask God for things, but God doesn't just bless us with our requests and ignore the other important areas of our lives. He prospers us in *all* areas, and this happens when we fight the good fight of faith.

During this hectic period, we heard about houses that were for sale outside the city. One caught my eye one day and my husband and I drove out to see it. It was located in the same area as the one that had burnt down. The property was beautiful in the pictures, but we knew we would need God to help us get it.

This five-bedroom home sat on one acre of land, and there was a second house on the property. The seller was also the builder, and we hit it off right away. The house had a unique layout with more bells and whistles than I had thought it would. It was a real gem.

At one point during the visit, I put my hand on a windowsill and a phrase came to my mind: "more than I could ask, think, or imagine."

Well, we left feeling very impressed. We would need to pray about it together.

Months went by and nothing changed substantially in our finances. Our finances actually looked pretty bad on paper. Everything that came in went out.

We had gotten my first book published, and now we did the same for my second one. To accomplish this, we had to go through months of financial planning and catch up on bills.

> DAY AFTER DAY, WE KEPT THE VISION BEFORE US.

So we just kept praising God. When we're stagnant in our faith, the harvest doesn't seem to flow as quickly. But when we're busy in our vision and moving quickly when God says to go, God's hand does move! Day after day, we kept the vision before us. Our bills always got paid—something at the last minute, but always on time. Loans were provided for, and we paid for all our school expenses and necessities. God took care of us.

One day, I saw that the house went off the market, but it hadn't been sold. So we just waited for God's next word. In the meantime, I posted pictures of it on my vision board, along with my confirmation scriptures. We just continued to thank God for it.

chapter nine

Exercising Yet Again!

WE SIGNED ANOTHER YEAR-LONG LEASE FOR OUR RENTAL HOUSE. I didn't like signing it, because I wanted to move. The more time went by, however, the more I just had to thank God and remain confident in Him.

But the days could be really tough and disheartening when there was no movement. Keeping our eyes focussed on God and not our natural circumstances can be difficult. Life is always changing, but it's so important not to get distracted by carnal things.

Sometimes we don't feel like reading the Bible, spending time in prayer, attending conferences, and listening to encouraging messages, but when we rise up and determine to keep growing our faith the benefits and blessings far outweigh the challenges.

If you're not moving forward, it may feel like you're just standing still. But in actuality you are moving backwards.

It was starting to get a little small in the house with our children growing and needing their own rooms, not to mention my parents needing their own space. I tried to organize our things and give away as much as I could, but especially during the winter it felt very tight.

It had been six months now since we'd taken the first step of going out to see that beautiful property, our "more than enough" home.

One day while driving to church, I got a notification on my phone about a new listing in the area where we were looking. Although the pictures made it seem unusual, the home had six bedrooms and seemed a good size for us.

Well, it sparked my interest. And when I saw that there was going to be an open house the following week, I heard a voice in my spirit say, "Go exercise your faith." So I got excited!

The open house was on a Sunday, so after church we took our whole family to go see it. Well, the pictures definitely hadn't shown how nice the house actually was. It had a great layout that made so much sense for our family. It wasn't huge, at least compared to the last one, but it had many things we liked. For instance, it was a raised bungalow so the basement had bright light and half our kids would be able to sleep down there, with the other two children being upstairs closer to us. The floors had a beautiful hardwood, I liked the colours, and overall it felt cozy and welcoming. Perhaps best of all, as we walked around we noticed that scriptures and faith messages had been painted on the walls. And the location couldn't be beat, close to the highway and only ten minutes from our children's school. With two and a half acres, it had a large garden, a greenhouse, and a firepit, and there would be room to add so much more.

It was wonderful to be there with our whole family and stand in agreement that we wanted to move into this house. It felt like the property was just for us, especially since no other families showed up for the open house.

Seeing that house was so important in our faith walk. When we don't exercise our faith, we tend to forget how to believe God for our prayers. We should never forget the seeds we've sown, and we shouldn't be afraid to step out and move like we've already received what He says we have.

We didn't have the cash or credit to purchase the house, but God didn't tell us we needed those things; we were tithers in the kingdom of God and He had promised to provide all our needs. The promises of God can be found throughout the Bible, and I believe that these promises are intended for us today.

> *For no matter how many promises God has made, they are "Yes" in Christ. And so through him the "Amen" is spoken by us to the glory of God.*
>
> —2 Corinthians 1:20

> *…so is my word that goes out from my mouth: it will not return to me empty, but will accomplish what I desire and achieve the purpose for which I sent it.*
>
> —Isaiah 55:11

When I prayed about my home, I spoke these scriptures, praising God and thanking Him for all He had done for me. Reading these words made my faith rise, which gave me encouragement, strength, and excitement for every area of my life. When we walk in godly confidence, we are able to see how easy it is to praise Him for everything in our lives. Our prayer times get more exciting and we become hopeful—first for ourselves, and then for others. People need *more* encouragement!

We went to see this house right before Christmas, and as a family we just kept thanking God that we were going to move in there. We prayed like it was already done.

This was also the same month my second book came out, and our ministry and business were both growing. Life was very demanding and exciting. In the meanwhile, we were listening to so many testimonies of God working in other people's lives—and we knew that what He does for others, He can do for us as well!

The time had come for us to enter into our Daniel fast. This is a three-week fast which comes from Daniel 10. Daniel, while seeking to gain understanding of a vision, prayed and humbled himself through fasting. God then heard his prayer, but the angel who was sent to give Daniel the answer to his prayer was held up by resistance; after twenty-one days, or three weeks, the angel was released to bring Daniel his answer.

Every year since starting our church, Danrey and I had done this fast and encouraged our congregation to do the same. I knew about fasting, of course, but it wasn't until I read Jentezen Franklin's book, *Fasting*,[2] that I really understood it. Once I understood that fasting wasn't just a religious exercise, I became very interested. I really wanted to fast and see God's hand move in my life; sometimes our routines, and specifically food, can block our communication with Him.

This year's Daniel fast was exceptionally exciting, and in our congregation most people were really hungry to see and experience God. For twenty-one nights, we hosted a time of prayer, praise, and encouragement at our church.

---

2   Jentezen Franklin, *Fasting* (Lake Mary, FL: Charisma House, 2008).

In the weeks before the fast, God had already been speaking to my spirit and showing me what to teach about in my midweek meetings. As I mentioned in the previous chapter, God had dropped the phrase "new wine" into my heart and I became so excited to share about this with the congregation.

Over the past few months, I felt that God had been preparing us. He was going to pour new wine into us!

As Christians, we need to recognize what's happening all around us and *know* and *trust* that God is working out all things for our good. As Romans 8:28 says, *"And we know that in all things God works for the good of those who love him, who have been called according to his purpose."*

With this message stirring in our hearts, I was also led to look into some other teachings from Jentezen Franklin to share with our midweek crew during the fast. What I stumbled upon confirmed everything God had been speaking to us about. He told me that when we fast, we get a new wineskin!

Equipped with a new wineskin, we were able to receive the new wine He was ready to pour out into us.

Up to this point, we had been regularly sowing financial seeds into our church building. God had put on our hearts a specific amount we were to give, and it was a big amount. We had been faithfully giving this amount for more than a year.

One evening during the fast, we added up all of our giving so far and wondered how much of our larger financial goal we had accomplished. We were surprised at the total, but the most surprising realization came when Danrey asked me, "What is the one-hundred-fold return on this amount?"

Now, I don't want people to get stuck on this. We know that God is our provider and not everything follows an exact formula. Christian nonsense has taken away from our ability to believe in God to fulfill the promises that have been written in the Bible.

However, the one-hundred-fold amount would cover the purchase price of the home we were looking to buy, and also allow us to pay off all of our outstanding debt.

"Yes, God!"

That's the first thing that came out of our mouths.

Then God said, "Now praise Me like you already have it!"

chapter ten

Blessed Life

LIVING A BLESSED LIFE DOESN'T MEAN YOU NECESSARILY HAVE everything you want every moment of the day and you never have to work again. To me, living a blessed life isn't about possessions or work. It's not about making sure our plans all work out the way I expect them to without anything ever going wrong. It's not about having the perfect family, the perfect job, the perfect marriage, or the perfect anything.

Living a blessed life is about having a stress-free, worry-free life full of the joy of the Lord. It's about knowing who created you, loves you, and always takes care of you. It's about not having to panic when you can't figure out what to do next, because you simply trust God to straighten your paths (Proverbs 3:5). It's about understanding that He who began a good work in you is carrying it to completion (Philippians 1:6). It's about living the Christian life as best we can and knowing that it is good.

If I'm doing my best to listen to the voice of God and walk with Him daily, He will lead and guide me and show me the way. Living a blessed life is knowing that I don't have to measure up to anyone else's standards, because God has made me with different talents and abilities than anyone else. God has given me my own journey, and through it I will get where He wants me to be. And He loves me enough to walk it out with me. He's with me each and every minute of the day. If I remind myself of that, I won't need to question every difficult circumstance I face. In fact, I can look at these trials and thank God that He has given me all the answers I need to navigate through them.

As a couple, Danrey and I kept growing in our faith. We kept taking steps together and trusting God. We may not have seen our house manifest yet, but God showed us so many other blessings and opportunities. We were happy, our children were happy, and we continued dreaming and imagining what was yet to come.

Our faith walk with Him caused us to step out of our comfort zone and believe for more than we ever had before. When the Bible calls us blessed, it means that God has pronounced a blessing upon us, His children, so that we can live free and prosperous lives. We are the seed of Abraham and can be prosperous in every area.

I say *can*, because we didn't believe for many years. We thought that God would give us our needs most of the time, but the rest of the time we had to struggle with our heads down. Humility isn't about accepting everything bad that comes our way, thinking of it as God's way of training us. Rather, humility is about positioning ourselves to listen to God and follow His leading.

When I started to believe that there had to be more to what God was saying to me in His Word, when I determined to read it for myself and realize that He was speaking to me through it, everything changed. I now believe that God is good and He wrote all the promises in the Bible for an important reason. I finally internalized the truth that God doesn't show favouritism; the healings and supernatural works He does for others, He will also do for me!

When our faith gets challenged, we tend to think that we must not be on the right path. This inevitably makes us feel frustrated and throws us off. But in fact the opposite is true: when there is opposition, when the pressure's on, that's usually a tell-tale sign that we're on the right path! Satan doesn't want us to realize that God is in control. He wants us to think that we don't need God. He wants to frustrate us and the plans God has for us. He wants us to think God's Word is ineffective. Meanwhile, the very trials we face are the ones God promises us that we can overcome. He wants our eyes to be on Him, for with Christ nothing is impossible.

After our church's Daniel fast, the pressure was on. Our spirits were ignited and Satan took notice. Although I had heard about demonic attacks before, I hadn't faced any. Over the years, however, I had been equipped with scripture in my heart and mind to stand up to these attacks, so when they occurred God was ready to work through me. Only through trials and pressure can we find out what we're made of. What comes out of our mouths during these times will demonstrate what is true in our lives (Matthew 15:18).

We read in 1 Peter 5:8 that Satan goes around like a roaring lion. What I didn't know is that this term—a roaring lion—is meant to refer to a really old lion that has no teeth. Well, this sparked such a revelation in me! When I hear this phrase, I now picture a lion that's so old, all he can do is roar. He can't bite, and so he uses his roar as a scare tactic. That's exactly what Satan does. He's going to make loud, scary noises, but that's *all* he can do. Get this straight in your heart!

During this time of crazy pressure and stress, God taught us how to be overcomers—and how to *stay* overcomers. He broke through in ways I had only imagined. New wine was being poured into me, along with other people in our church who were reaching for the next level and stopping at nothing to get there. The church grew immensely. God spoke to so many people right where they were, each in their own personal ways.

One day, I had a prophetic dream. I was walking beside the ocean when a huge wave came over me. But as it flowed over me, I was able to keep breathing and walk out the other side. I wasn't afraid. That spoke to exactly what I had been going through. I knew that God's strength would enable me to get to the other side of this challenge, unharmed and unafraid.

I had another dream, this time of a really large aircraft. Like, strangely large. It flew down out of the sky and landed right in front of me and many people from our church. The plane was blue and white.

> GOD TAUGHT US HOW TO BE OVERCOMERS—AND HOW TO *STAY* OVERCOMERS.

The next day, I couldn't stop thinking about this dream, looking for the spiritual meaning. In my spirit, I came to understand that the plane represented a large organization that was highly powered by the Holy Spirit. The colours, too, were prophetic, speaking to authority, purity, and victory.

While doing laundry that day, I heard God say that He was going to take me to the nations. I was concerned, because I didn't want to spend too much time away from my children, but God assured me that He would accomplish it through the books I was writing. At this point, I was surprised that

God had kept giving me the desire to write books. I hadn't thought I would ever be an author. My only goal had been to encourage people.

I started having many dreams about blessings and prosperity, and through these revelations I felt excited and overwhelmed.

Many opportunities soon presented themselves in our business and ministry, giving us the choice of whether to take them. As God opened these new doors, we were able to move into new positions. And we were equipped to succeed and thrive in every area. God was pushing us forward, and we knew this path would bring many blessings—including our new home.

We continued to look at houses and pray over the ones we liked. Our faith was growing, our vision was expanding, and we believed God was up to something. We just had to be patient and never lose hope.

One day, our landlord wanted to meet with us. He asked about when my parents would be moving out, since they had been looking to get their own place again. He felt that the amount of rent we were paying was far too low.

In boldness, and perhaps frustration, Danrey then asked if the landlord wanted to sell the home to us. This caught him totally off-guard.

A few days later, the landlord called us and his tone had changed. He had been talking to his wife and they loved the idea of selling to us. They even offered to help us with the down-payment.

Our heads were spinning a bit. We hadn't really thought of living there much longer, but we realized the situation would feel different if we owned it.

What had just happened?

Soon my parents came to us with their own news. They had found a really nice apartment and would be moving out in a few months. The ball was definitely rolling.

One of our concerns was the amount of time we currently spent driving to and from church and the children's schools every day. To meet this challenge, we decided to sell our van and replace it with two smaller vehicles. This was a major step for us, because we owed a lot of money on the van and wanted to be out of debt.

After the van sold, my husband came home with a small six-seater minivan. This would allow us to still take an upcoming trip we had been planning for. We packed minimally, and we saved money on gas.

Our faith grew on that trip. We enjoyed every moment and developed a clearer picture of how God had been working in every area of our lives.

When we got back home, the landlord wanted to meet up with us again and talk about the next steps in the process of buying the house. Because of the sale of the van, we now had $10,000 in our account and offered that as a down-payment. Next we just needed to wait for the house to be assessed. From there, we could figure out how to handle the mortgage.

I still believed God for what it says in Deuteronomy 6:11: *"houses filled with all kinds of good things you did not provide…"* I never gave up on the dream of owning a home, debt-free. Buying this house didn't seem like the way to achieve that, but it was still *a* way. I trusted God to work out all things for our good.

We hadn't told our parents about this plan, although we pictured telling them one day when they came over. But when I spoke to my dad on the phone one day, I felt compelled to tell him about this opportunity. He thought the right thing was definitely to get the house appraised. He then offered us another $10,000, since the bigger the down-payment, the better.

I didn't know what to say! I hadn't ever asked my dad for money like that. He had paid for some of my college education and had supported me in every endeavour, but this offer left me speechless. He was part of God's setup.

In the meantime, we were still looking at houses outside the city, since our heart's desire was still to own an acreage.

Weeks passed and I continued to show interest in some of the houses that were posted for sale outside the city. Danrey and I often drove to see the properties, but nothing ever seemed to be quite right. Perhaps the house had been built on great land but faced a whole bunch of neighbours, or maybe there weren't many neighbours but the roads were terrible, or the houses looked smaller than in the pictures or there wasn't enough land for being out in the country…

There were a lot of factors to take into consideration.

One day while praying and thanking God, I was reminded of a farmhouse I had once seen in a photo. God brought it to mind and reminded me that we still had the option to build. Why had I been limiting my thinking? Not only could we build a home, but we could build one like the farmhouse in that picture!

That's My House

My spirit got excited as I thought about designing a house. It could have the right number of rooms, the exact style I wanted, and even the landscaping and privacy I was looking for. This became my new prayer, for God to bring into my path a homebuilder. It would have to be the right one. A God setup.

During this time, we got a phone call from our landlord. He let us know that the house we were living in would soon be assessed, and after that we'd know how much it would cost to purchase.

The assessment got done and the papers came in just a few days before we were scheduled to take a faith trip to Texas. We had been invited to attend a conference with Jerry Savelle Ministries, and we were more than excited to go. We knew that we would be filled up there and spend that time in an atmosphere that would grow our faith. We had to go!

The assessment on the house was $335,000, and the landlord wanted to sell it to us for $345,000. They would hold the mortgage for us, and we would be able to avoid paying a lot of extra expenses.

We felt it was very nice of them to offer us this opportunity, but I was excited to see what God would do next. After all, He had been the one who said that He would give us houses, that we weren't to go into any more debt. He was our provider.

The landlord told us that he would like to sell it to us in the new year, which gave us a few months to take all the steps God wanted us to take.

chapter eleven

Back to Basics

THE BIBLE TALKS ABOUT THE SEED TIME AND HARVEST TIME, AND I knew that after planting so many seeds in my life the harvest was going to be greater than I could imagine. As the Lord declares in Amos 9:14: *"The days are coming... when the reaper will be overtaken by the plowman and the planter by the one treading grapes."*

After our church's Daniel fast, I found myself asking God, "What do You want me to teach people now?" I thought that it would have to be something exceptionally revolutionary.

And it was. He told me to go back to basics.

A lot of times, we can get so caught up in all the exciting spiritual things going on around us that it feels tedious just to sit down and read the Bible. Our prayer time can feel ordinary and we may start to feel bored.

After a fast, though, you start thinking, acting, and expecting differently. Yet it's so important to go back and continue to do the regular, foundational things, because in doing them *new* things will be revealed. You'll read and pray with a different insight and hunger. Your foundation will be strengthened.

God's Word stays the same, but we don't understand everything in it. He needs to reveal things to us when we're ready so that we can grow and change. We are all on a journey.

This is also true in terms of finances. At church I was led to teach about handling our finances according to God's way, and the importance of going back to the simplicity of practicing diligence and being good stewards. It's so important to pray over the finances that go in and out of our hands every day.

After a few nights of hearing these great messages again, Danrey and I went out to buy gas for the car. I only had $10 on me, so I looked at my husband and we prayed over the situation. As we thanked God for it, an overwhelming joy came over us. It was supernatural. We felt an unreal amount of peace.

We went home that night to find more than $500 waiting for us. God is so good!

That same week, we sat down and wrote out our monthly budgets, praying over them together. I've always been the one in our marriage to take care of the finances for our home, ministry, and business. It comes naturally to me and I enjoy it. But this time my husband took on a different role. God was stirring his heart and I knew we need to be in agreement.

So much favour came to us, including our church rent, our home rent, and business bills. We knew this was because we were being diligent to pray for everything, allowing God to work on our behalf. We had a shortage in our personal budget of about $1,000—but just two days after we gave our budget over to God and thanked Him, we received more than enough.

While looking for new ways to bring in extra income, I saw an ad for a large Christian ministry with which we had previously partnered. I thought that maybe I could join their prayer team or call centre. My challenge was to create a resume, cover letter, and written testimony. It had been eighteen years since I'd needed to apply for a job like this! I found a website to help me and even had to pay $30 to gain their expertise.

The very next day, I got a phone call from the Canadian headquarters of that ministry. The woman I spoke with was very encouraging, and although I didn't live in their province she informed me that she'd keep my resume in a special file since I was the exact type of person they were looking for. They were very encouraged with my testimony, and she suggested that I record it.

I was completely overwhelmed by this news. Although it wasn't what I had been looking for, it was definitely an open door. God was setting things up and I knew there would be so much more to this opportunity.

> WE KEPT THE BIG PICTURE IN MIND AND CONTINUED TO PUSH OURSELVES.

When COVID-19 hit the world, we had been busy paying off loans and expenses as we could. We were eager to see the big vision of our dreams come true, but we knew it would take a lot of little steps to get there. But we kept the big picture in mind and continued to push ourselves. That's the word God had given me: *push*.

During the pandemic, while the church building itself had to shut its doors to large gatherings, we had to think of creative ways to connect and encourage all the people around us. We needed encouragement, too, but we knew we would reap the harvest God had promised us. We were digging in our heels, diving into the Word, and spending more and more time with God.

We were at the church one day doing paperwork and filming video encouragements when I received a call from that large ministry I had sent my resume to. They wanted to connect and send out resources our church may need, at no cost. Another reason for their call was that they wanted permission to use my testimony in an upcoming ad campaign that would be released across Canada in 2021. What an honour! Of course I said yes. I discovered that they would be sending out a crew in a few months to record my testimony.

That open door just kept widening!

During this time of new connection, I finished writing a book about marriage. Even when I thought life couldn't get any busier, God found ways to spark the excitement in my heart to share about His power and love through writing.

As we pray and exercise our faith, God puts desires in our hearts. He then uses these opportunities to help us grow. For Danrey and myself, our faith has grown in every way since stepping out to believe for impossible things. We just had to focus on the prize, and there were many more prizes to be won.

Physically, we will never be the same. Spiritually, we will never be the same. Relationally, we will never be the same. Mentally, we will never be the same. We have changed and grown. God is taking us from glory to glory, all through the application of *simple* faith.

Over and over, we had to tell ourselves, "Just believe." We often reminded ourselves what God says and what we believe. This never changes, no matter what stage you're at in your Christian walk. By taking one step after another, soon enough you arrive at the destination you've been dreaming about…

only it's *way* better than what you asked for, thought, or imagined. And the journey is the most important part of all.

During the pandemic, my ears were so tuned to believing in and receiving our debt-free farm home that I could hear it everywhere I went. For example, I got further confirmation one day while watching a message from Jesse Duplantis, who said, "You have it *because* it's impossible!" I was familiar with the verse that tells that nothing is impossible for God, but my faith was brought to a whole new level by turning that verse around and believing that I have what I need *because* it's impossible.

When we encountered car troubles, I thought about the fact that the vehicle we drove wasn't exactly the one I had been praying for. Then God said to me, "Will you let Me now bring your vehicle to you?"

"But God," I said, "You tell us to go out and get things, too. So I'm confused."

My head and heart were quickly corrected. This time, God was saying to me that He was going to bring it.

Okay, Lord, I prayed. *Thank You. I have peace.*

chapter twelve

Double Portion

We kept looking for houses outside the city. One listing we saw was for a small home about a minute outside the city limits, but it was on five acres. Our initial thought was that we could cram our family into this little house and live in it while we built the home of our dreams right next door. We felt like this might be the best option.

At this time, we were very busy at church, and soon Christmas came. Then we found another listing, this one for a larger home that had been freshly renovated—but it was only on one acre.

This, too, seemed like a good option. It might not have been exactly what we wanted, but it would fit our family and we loved the area.

One day, Danrey and I took a drive out to this house. He had felt an urging in his spirit to pray over it as we drove by. Afterward we drove to the other home we had looked at, which was only a short distance away, and prayed over that one too.

What were we doing? We didn't know.

As we praised and worshipped God, we received a word from God: "Why not both?" Oh my goodness! We were struck speechless at the thought of potentially owning both properties. We could live and enjoy the one that was move-in ready, and have our offices in the smaller house. And eventually we could start to build our own farmhouse.

We now thanked God for acquiring both properties, and trusted Him to lead and guide us to that outcome.

At this point, we actively started giving away furniture and selling some of our things in preparation for our move, even though nothing had been finalized yet.

By January 2021, we were fasting—as we did at the start of every year—to hear from God. This year, God placed it on my heart to give more. So I took out my new agenda and began to write down our financial plans. But then God stopped me and said, "Don't write down your debt." When I heard this, I knew it was going to be a *new* season.

As we prayed about our giving, God gave us a huge financial challenge: to give, believing that we would see our vision manifest very quickly. Our giving multiplied to amounts we had never dreamed of.

We read in 2 Corinthians 9:10, *"Now he who supplies seed to the sower and bread for food will also supply and increase your store of seed and will enlarge the harvest of your righteousness."* If you understand that He has given you a seed to sow, it's easy to give it.

We have to realize that we can sow seeds with what we currently have. We don't have to wait to see what may come across our path. That's not faith. We need to give from what we have, thanking God for blessing it. The things we have been given by God aren't ours; they are His, and we are called to be good stewards. You can't keep what isn't yours. If you do, the flow will stop.

For twenty-one days, we multiplied our seeds daily. We had to believe for the *big* amounts to come our way, then give them as fast as they came in, with God directing where it was all to go!

Day 1	We sowed $1. (We also paid off a credit card.)
Day 2	We sowed $2.
Day 3	We sowed $4.
Day 4	We sowed $8.
Day 5	We sowed $16.
Day 6	We sowed $32.
Day 7	We sowed $64.

On the seventh day, we took a drive to see our homes again… but this time Danrey drove a little further down the road than we had on previous visits. We saw a property here that we hadn't seen before, and our eyes enlarged as we took it in.

He spoke first: "Look at that house! That is our house."

As we drove past it again, I was speechless. It was exactly like the farmhouse I had seen in that old picture, but standing right before me in real life on the nicest of lots.

After seeing that property, my prayer got a little fuzzy. I added that home's address to our vision board and just kept thanking God every day for our beautiful debt-free home.

Day 8	We sowed $128.
Day 9	We sowed $256.
Day 10	We sowed $512.

From the eleventh day to the twenty-first, we thanked and praised God as we committed to supporting two other ministers. We also sowed smaller seeds to other outreaches.

When the fast ended, Danrey awoke in the morning and told me that God had given him a vision: He was going to accelerate us.

As I prayed that day, a devotion came up on my social media feed called "Fasting for Your Goals," by Terri Savelle Foy. I was surprised at the title, since it confirmed everything I believed. We were on the right track!

The months went by and we continued to pray, believe, and listen. For a long time we didn't see any doors open for these properties.

When we questioned God's silence in it all, we were brought back to remembering a time when it had seemed like things *were* moving—when God had given us the opportunity to purchase the house we currently lived in. As we got our finances in order, we saw that we would actually do it—if that's what we wanted.

No, this rental house wasn't like the homes on my vision board, but we felt like buying it was the right step to take, one that would bring us into the next level of operating in our faith. We had gotten caught up in looking for the perfect home in the perfect place, and in the process we strayed off the path that had been opened for us supernaturally. And it had been opened to us the previous year, right when we'd prayed! We had so much favour with the landlord that we'd forgotten that God had been the one to set it up for us.

It was exciting to get back on track and focus on what had been in front of us the whole time.

As we discussed the next steps for us to take, we were also blessed with a cabin we had been praying for. This cabin was being sold by friends of ours, and they had allowed us to go stay in it for a week. It was very large and our whole extended family could fit into it. The next thing we knew, my in-laws got the vision that it would be a perfect place for them to purchase for their "children's children."

This wasn't the way I had thought everything was going to happen, but it was much better! The vision now included our entire family. This was the double portion—a house and a cabin for us to enjoy along with peace and a vision for everything else our hearts desired!

I was getting very excited about this whole vision board thing. We were sowing seeds into other ministries and physically seeing our dreams and goals get checked off.

At this time, our eldest son was attending a Christian private school and we had believed that it would be paid off by May... and it was. That checkmark was particularly exciting. We were celebrating both the big and small things.

We are now living in a home that isn't financed by a bank but rather through the generosity and kindness of people. The amount of money we pay each month is the same amount we paid when renting, but now the paperwork says that the house is ours.

I really hadn't thought I would be so happy purchasing the rental home, but that's the overflow of God. When He gives you a vision, He also brings the provision.

We are paying off this home in cash. We are also paying off our family van in cash. It feels so good to get rid of debt.

As Romans 13:8 tells us, *"Let no debt remain outstanding, except the continuing debt to love one another..."*

For now, I'm going to take care of that which is under my care and enjoy being in our current home. We will know when it's time to move or build our next home. In the meantime, I want to show people the Kingdom of God, since I know that the seeds we sow produce a harvest. Maybe this house is going to be a seed that can one day be given to someone else. That is so exciting to me!

On our vision board is land. We're still sowing seeds to purchase a property where we can build our dream farmhouse. Every day I look at the farmhouse picture I found years ago, thanking God for the home we have as well as the home we will one day have. I can believe for both, as well as all the other things on my vision board and in my heart. God is teaching us not to place limits on our beliefs.

Part Two

God's Word Over Our Finances

When Danrey and I started our faith walk, we proclaimed God's Word over our finances whether or not we fully believed it. Day after day, those scriptures became part of us, and through this process our minds were renewed to better appreciate God's will for His children. When the phone rings, we don't worry that it's a creditor calling.

As we proclaimed God's Word, we began to change from the inside-out. Then our finances changed, too.

It wasn't instant, though. It took perseverance and growth on our part. Some of it took years to walk out. But having God's Word right in front of us, letting His Spirit guide us, became the most exciting and rewarding part of our lives. We didn't need to physically see the promises and dreams manifest for us to know that those promises and dreams were ours. We had faith that they were.

I want to encourage you to know that God will give you the desires of your heart. He put those desires in you and provides them all. If you take the first step and believe that God is your provider and tithe, or just start giving, you open the door of faith!

I realized that the more I trusted God with our finances and took steps of faith, the easier it became to believe and know that I have been healed, set free, delivered, saved, transformed, and made new. Trusting God in your finances will give you an unshakable foundation for every other area of your life. I can't live and love Him without giving.

The biggest thing God showed us through these years of standing in faith for a house is to never stop believing. Never stop believing that God has more than you can ask, think, or imagine. Never stop dreaming and pursuing your dreams.

As we walk by faith, we strengthen our walk in Him by believing for things we cannot do on our own. By reading the Word, praying, and declaring His truth over our lives, we build our relationship with God. We see many amazing things happen, and not just our own prayers being answered; we receive many blessings by becoming the conduit for other people's miracles and faith growth.

Here is the test: how do we react when we see others receiving things we would like in our own lives? Do we get jealous? Do we compare and start to think that maybe God loves them more than He loves us? Do we conclude that we aren't doing enough to please Him?

These thoughts come from a mentality of fear. When we operate in fear, our vision is blocked. Fear tells us that God is selective and doesn't really care about us. Fear tells us that He withholds good things from us. Fear tells us that we will never see our prayers answered.

Fear comes into our lives when we take our eyes off God and His plan for our us. Fear comes when our relationship with God isn't strong.

But according to 1 John 4:18, perfect love casts out all fear. We have to look to God every day and be filled with His perfect love. As we meditate on how much God loves us, we will see and know that He is good and rewards those who diligently seek Him. He has released so many blessings to you already. All you have to do is grab them—by faith.

My faith has grown because I allowed myself to dream big!

Sometimes you have to actively pursue your dreams in order to start believing for the rest of your life. God cares about your entire being! If you can believe God in one area, you can believe in all the others. As you pursue one area, pause for a moment and appreciate all the other things He is lining up for you as well!

In this next part of the book, I want to encourage you to write out a series of powerful scriptures for you to meditate on. I would also encourage you to the take time at the beginning of each week to write down one scripture along with your goals, seeds, and harvest.

Commit all your ways to God and you will have great success! Jerry Savelle always says that if you're willing to wait forever, it won't take very long. I like that. It really takes the pressure off you and keeps you confident in Christ.

As you write these verses down, personalize them for yourself. Look up the different translations that are available and meditate on them. Declare them out loud. God's Word has power!

You got this!

Week 1

Dear friend, I pray that you may enjoy good health and that all may go well with you, even as your soul is getting along well.
—3 John 2

_____

_____

_____

_____

_____

_____

_____

_____

_____

_____

Week 2

A good person leaves an inheritance for their children's children, but a sinner's wealth is stored up for the righteous.
—Proverbs 13:22

Week 3

I will make you into a great nation, and I will bless you; I will make your name great, and you will be a blessing. I will bless those who bless you, and whoever curses you I will curse; and all peoples on earth will be blessed through you.

—Genesis 12:2–3

Week 4

The blessing of the Lord brings wealth, without painful toil for it.
—Proverbs 10:22

Week 5

What the wicked dread will overtake them; what the righteous desire will be granted.

—Proverbs 10:24

Week 6

When the Lord your God brings you into the land he swore to your fathers, to Abraham, Isaac and Jacob, to give you—a land with large, flourishing cities you did not build, houses filled with all kinds of good things you did not provide, wells you did not dig, and vineyards and olive groves you did not plant...
—Deuteronomy 6:10–11

Week 7

For the Lord your God is bringing you into a good land—a land with brooks, streams, and deep springs gushing out into the valleys and hills; a land with wheat and barley, vines and fig trees, pomegranates, olive oil and honey; a land where bread will not be scarce and you will lack nothing...

—Deuteronomy 8:7–9

_____

_____

_____

_____

_____

_____

_____

_____

Week 8

But remember the Lord your God, for it is he who gives you the ability to produce wealth, and so confirms his covenant, which he swore to your ancestors, as it is today.

—Deuteronomy 8:18

_____

_____

_____

_____

_____

_____

_____

_____

_____

Week 9

However, there need be no poor people among you, for in the land the Lord your God is giving you to possess as your inheritance, he will richly bless you...

—Deuteronomy 15:4

_____

_____

_____

_____

_____

_____

_____

_____

_____

Week 10

Christ redeemed us from the curse of the law by becoming a curse for us, for it is written: "Cursed is everyone who is hung on a pole." He redeemed us in order that the blessing given to Abraham might come to the Gentiles through Christ Jesus, so that by faith we might receive the promise of the Spirit.

—Galatians 3:13–14

Week 11

If you fully obey the Lord your God and carefully follow all his commands I give you today, the Lord your God will set you high above all the nations on earth. All these blessings will come on you and accompany you if you obey the Lord your God:

You will be blessed in the city and blessed in the country.

The fruit of your womb will be blessed, and the crops of your land and the young of your livestock—the calves of your herds and the lambs of your flocks.

Your basket and your kneading trough will be blessed.

You will be blessed when you come in and blessed when you go out.

The Lord will grant that the enemies who rise up against you will be defeated before you. They will come at you from one direction but flee from you in seven.

The Lord will send a blessing on your barns and on everything you put your hand to. The Lord your God will bless you in the land he is giving you.

The Lord will establish you as his holy people, as he promised you on oath, if you keep the commands of the Lord your God and walk in obedience to him. Then all the peoples on earth will see that you are called by the name of the Lord, and they will fear you. The Lord will grant you abundant prosperity—in the fruit of your womb, the young of your livestock and the crops of your ground—in the land he swore to your ancestors to give you.

God's Word Over Our Finances

The Lord will open the heavens, the storehouse of his bounty, to send rain on your land in season and to bless all the work of your hands. You will lend to many nations but will borrow from none. The Lord will make you the head, not the tail. If you pay attention to the commands of the Lord your God that I give you this day and carefully follow them, you will always be at the top, never at the bottom. Do not turn aside from any of the commands I give you today, to the right or to the left, following other gods and serving them.

—Deuteronomy 28:1–14

Week 12

The wife of a man from the company of the prophets cried out to Elisha, "Your servant my husband is dead, and you know that he revered the Lord. But now his creditor is coming to take my two boys as his slaves."

Elisha replied to her, "How can I help you? Tell me, what do you have in your house?"

"Your servant has nothing there at all," she said, "except a small jar of olive oil."

Elisha said, "Go around and ask all your neighbors for empty jars. Don't ask for just a few. 4 Then go inside and shut the door behind you and your sons. Pour oil into all the jars, and as each is filled, put it to one side."

She left him and shut the door behind her and her sons. They brought the jars to her and she kept pouring. When all the jars were full, she said to her son, "Bring me another one."

But he replied, "There is not a jar left." Then the oil stopped flowing.

She went and told the man of God, and he said, "Go, sell the oil and pay your debts. You and your sons can live on what is left."

—2 Kings 4:1–7

_____

_____

God's Word Over Our Finances

Week 13

This is what the Lord says—your Redeemer, the Holy One of Israel: "I am the Lord your God, who teaches you what is best for you, who directs you in the way you should go."

—Isaiah 48:17

Week 14

He who did not spare his own Son, but gave him up for us all—how will he not also, along with him, graciously give us all things?

—Romans 8:32

Week 15

His divine power has given us everything we need for a godly life through our knowledge of him who called us by his own glory and goodness. Through these he has given us his very great and precious promises, so that through them you may participate in the divine nature, having escaped the corruption in the world caused by evil desires.

—2 Peter 1:3–4

_____

_____

_____

_____

_____

_____

_____

_____

Week 16

For he has rescued us from the dominion of darkness and brought us into the kingdom of the Son he loves...
—Colossians 1:13

Week 17

What I am saying is that as long as an heir is underage, he is no different from a slave, although he owns the whole estate. The heir is subject to guardians and trustees until the time set by his father. So also, when we were underage, we were in slavery under the elemental spiritual forces of the world. But when the set time had fully come, God sent his Son, born of a woman, born under the law, to redeem those under the law, that we might receive adoption to sonship. Because you are his sons, God sent the Spirit of his Son into our hearts, the Spirit who calls out, "Abba, Father." So you are no longer a slave, but God's child; and since you are his child, God has made you also an heir.

—Galatians 4:1–7

_____

_____

_____

_____

_____

_____

Week 18

Looking at his disciples, he said: "Blessed are you who are poor, for yours is the kingdom of God."

—Luke 6:20[3]

_____

_____

_____

_____

_____

_____

_____

_____

_____

[3] No, I didn't make a mistake with this one. The disciples, for example, were poor, so they humbly came and trusted in God.

Week 19

The Spirit of the Lord is on me, because he has anointed me to proclaim good news to the poor. He has sent me to proclaim freedom for the prisoners and recovery of sight for the blind, to set the oppressed free, to proclaim the year of the Lord's favor.
—Luke 4:18–19

Week 20

...and provide for those who grieve in Zion—to bestow on them a crown of beauty instead of ashes, the oil of joy instead of mourning, and a garment of praise instead of a spirit of despair. They will be called oaks of righteousness, a planting of the Lord for the display of his splendor.

They will rebuild the ancient ruins and restore the places long devastated; they will renew the ruined cities that have been devastated for generations. Strangers will shepherd your flocks; foreigners will work your fields and vineyards. And you will be called priests of the Lord, you will be named ministers of our God. You will feed on the wealth of nations, and in their riches you will boast.

Instead of your shame you will receive a double portion, and instead of disgrace you will rejoice in your inheritance. And so you will inherit a double portion in your land, and everlasting joy will be yours.

"For I, the Lord, love justice; I hate robbery and wrongdoing. In my faithfulness I will reward my people and make an everlasting covenant with them. Their descendants will be known among the nations and their offspring among the peoples. All who see them will acknowledge that they are a people the Lord has blessed."

—Isaiah 61:3–9

That's My House

Week 21

No one can serve two masters. Either you will hate the one and love the other, or you will be devoted to the one and despise the other. You cannot serve both God and money.

—Matthew 6:24

Week 22

Do not be afraid, little flock, for your Father has been pleased to give you the kingdom. Sell your possessions and give to the poor. Provide purses for yourselves that will not wear out, a treasure in heaven that will never fail, where no thief comes near and no moth destroys. For where your treasure is, there your heart will be also.

—Luke 12:32–34

Week 23

Cast all your anxiety on him because he cares for you.
—I Peter 5:7

Week 24

Who, then, are those who fear the Lord? He will instruct them in the ways they should choose. They will spend their days in prosperity, and their descendants will inherit the land.
—Psalm 25:12–13

Week 25

Blessed are all who fear the Lord, who walk in obedience to him. You will eat the fruit of your labor; blessings and prosperity will be yours.

—Psalm 128:1–2

Week 26

And my God will meet all your needs according to the riches of his glory in Christ Jesus.

—Philippians 4:19

Week 27

Come to me, all you who are weary and burdened, and I will give you rest. Take my yoke upon you and learn from me, for I am gentle and humble in heart, and you will find rest for your souls. For my yoke is easy and my burden is light.
—Matthew 11:28–30

Week 28

The Lord is my shepherd, I lack nothing... You prepare a table before me in the presence of my enemies. You anoint my head with oil; my cup overflows.

—Psalm 23:1, 5

Week 29

"For I know the plans I have for you," declares the Lord, "plans to prosper you and not to harm you, plans to give you hope and a future."

—Jeremiah 29:11

Week 30

So he got up and went to his father.

But while he was still a long way off, his father saw him and was filled with compassion for him; he ran to his son, threw his arms around him and kissed him.

The son said to him, "Father, I have sinned against heaven and against you. I am no longer worthy to be called your son."

But the father said to his servants, "Quick! Bring the best robe and put it on him. Put a ring on his finger and sandals on his feet. Bring the fattened calf and kill it. Let's have a feast and celebrate. For this son of mine was dead and is alive again; he was lost and is found.' So they began to celebrate.

—Luke 15:20–24

Week 31

No, in all these things we are more than conquerors through him who loved us.

—Romans 8:37

Week 32

Jesus looked at them and said, "With man this is impossible, but with God all things are possible."
—Matthew 19:26

Week 33

If any of you lacks wisdom, you should ask God, who gives generously to all without finding fault, and it will be given to you.
—James 1:5

Week 34

...for, "Who has known the mind of the Lord so as to instruct him?" But we have the mind of Christ.

—I Corinthians 2:16

_____

_____

_____

_____

_____

_____

_____

_____

_____

_____

Week 35

Is anyone among you in trouble? Let them pray. Is anyone happy? Let them sing songs of praise.

—James 5:13

Week 36

Ask and it will be given to you; seek and you will find; knock and the door will be opened to you.

—Matthew 7:7

_____

_____

_____

_____

_____

_____

_____

_____

_____

Week 37

When the Lord restored the fortunes of Zion, we were like those who dreamed. Our mouths were filled with laughter, our tongues with songs of joy. Then it was said among the nations, "The Lord has done great things for them." The Lord has done great things for us, and we are filled with joy.

Restore our fortunes, Lord, like streams in the Negev. Those who sow with tears will reap with songs of joy. Those who go out weeping, carrying seed to sow, will return with songs of joy, carrying sheaves with them.

—Psalm 126:1–6

Week 38

From the fruit of their mouth a person's stomach is filled; with the harvest of their lips they are satisfied.

—Proverbs 18:20

Week 39

Let us not become weary in doing good, for at the proper time we will reap a harvest if we do not give up.
—Galatians 6:9

Week 40

Great peace have those who love your law, and nothing can make them stumble.

—Psalm 119:165

Week 41

He determines the number of the stars and calls them each by name.

—Psalm 147:4

Week 42

When the Lord takes pleasure in anyone's way, he causes their enemies to make peace with them.

—Proverbs 16:7

_____

_____

_____

_____

_____

_____

_____

_____

_____

Week 43

One person gives freely, yet gains even more; another withholds unduly, but comes to poverty. A generous person will prosper; whoever refreshes others will be refreshed.

—Proverbs 11:24–25

_____

_____

_____

_____

_____

_____

_____

_____

_____

Week 44

Honor the Lord with your wealth, with the firstfruits of all your crops; then your barns will be filled to overflowing, and your vats will brim over with new wine.

—Proverbs 3:9–10

_____

_____

_____

_____

_____

_____

_____

_____

Week 45

The plans of the diligent lead to profit as surely as haste leads to poverty.

—Proverbs 21:5

Week 46

"Bring the whole tithe into the storehouse, that there may be food in my house. Test me in this," says the Lord Almighty, "and see if I will not throw open the floodgates of heaven and pour out so much blessing that there will not be room enough to store it."
—Malachi 3:10

Week 47

Give, and it will be given to you. A good measure, pressed down, shaken together and running over, will be poured into your lap. For with the measure you use, it will be measured to you.
—Luke 6:38

Week 48

For you know the grace of our Lord Jesus Christ, that though he was rich, yet for your sake he became poor, so that you through his poverty might become rich.

—2 Corinthians 8:9

Week 49

Remember this: Whoever sows sparingly will also reap sparingly, and whoever sows generously will also reap generously.
—2 Corinthians 9:6

Week 50

Now to him who is able to do immeasurably more than all we ask or imagine, according to his power that is at work within us, to him be glory in the church and in Christ Jesus throughout all generations, for ever and ever! Amen.
—Ephesians 3:20

Week 51

...so is my word that goes out from my mouth: it will not return to me empty, but will accomplish what I desire and achieve the purpose for which I sent it.

—Isaiah 55:11

Week 52

For the revelation awaits an appointed time; it speaks of the end and will not prove false. Though it linger, wait for it; it will certainly come and will not delay.

—Habakkuk 2:3

Also by the Author

Marriage Uncut
978-1-4866-2044-9

A little girl dreams of her wedding day, not her marriage. She probably doesn't even know what the word marriage means—just how much crinoline she wants under her dress. At least this is what Christie was thinking about, not the marriage relationship, money matters, or faith decisions.

In the first half of this book, Christie shares of the real-life decisions and dramas that occurred before—and after—she and her husband said "I do." In the second half, she breaks down the pre-marriage and marriage classes her ministry shares with other couples.

Be encouraged as Christie and her husband share with you their most intimate and vulnerable experiences. Love is a choice, and through love you can forgive, hope, and give your marriage an exciting and fulfilling future.

The Promised Child
978-1-4866-1649-7

Danrey and Christie Amoyo knew that they wanted to be parents, but when their happy announcement turned into the worst possible scenario they found out that becoming parents was not to be an easy path for them.

This book is a written testimony of how determination, coming from a new revelation of faith, can change lives. It will demonstrate that the promises we read about in the Bible are for us today, even if we don't yet know how they apply to the situations we're living through.

Be encouraged by the Amoyos' experience as, after years of heartbreak and loss, the Word becomes real and they put their faith first.

Crayons, Crumbs, and Christian Growth
ISBN: 978-1-4866-1714-2

Parenting children is a wonderful blessing that comes with great challenges. As you navigate the waters of parenthood, it can be easy to feel disconnected from life and your faith. You may think you are alone on this journey, and you may be frustrated trying to meet the demands all around you.

But these years can be the greatest of your life—years in which God shows you how real He is, how faith actually works, and how you can enjoy the blessings He's given you. In *Crayons, Crumbs, and Christian Growth*, Christie shares about how the trials and treasures of parenting her own children has taught her so much about who God is.

www.ingramcontent.com/pod-product-compliance
Lightning Source LLC
LaVergne TN
LVHW051522070426
835507LV00023B/3258